Logistics of Industrial Enterprise

Logistics Research

Dr (Er) Om Prakash

Professor and Chairman (T&P)

SMS Lucknow

Logistics of Industrial Enterprise

Introduction

Evolution of logistics has its roots from the military operations, and the concepts have been emerged from some of Peter Drucker's descriptions and treatise on economics (Drucker, 1962). Logistics had its crucial importance in military operations, where a critical network exists or created to supply goods or information or utilities from one location of its source to one or more or a chain of destinations (Weele, 2002). A fair amount of success of military operations was dependent on the successful logistics plan and execution. Today the growth of logistics significance realization has accelerated to the level that it is being regarded as a key business performance parameter by top enterprises.

Logistics is a business process which involves multiple departments in its operations and so it cuts across functional boundaries and expects the required contribution from each department. For instance, departments like marketing, finance, operations and accounts could be involved in varying degree of interactions. Historically, logistics evolved in four phases as represented in the figure below (TSENG *et al.*, 2005):

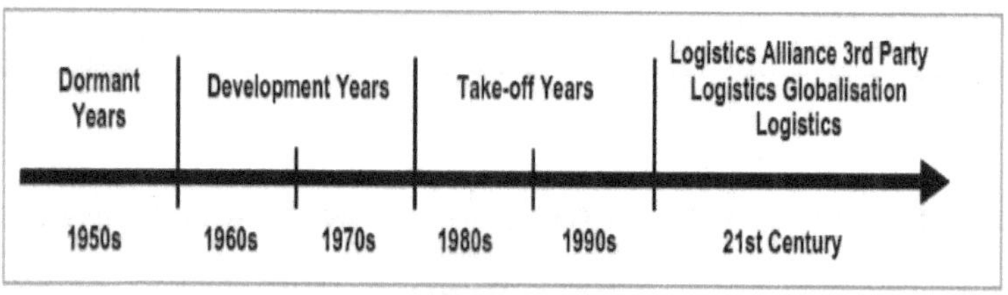

Logistics historical development

Source: Logistic Evolution (TSENG *et al.*, 2005)

From the dormant stages, or specialized to only military operations, to its gradual cognizance in the second stage, followed by realization and take-off years, where the new ideas on business were assimilated, to the latest trends in logistics, partnership with 3rd parties in supply chain and effects of Globalization on logistics, the evolution has been phenomenal (Chang, 1998). In the current stage of development, it is realized that the logistics requires interactions with the external supply chain interlinking a complex path from supplier to destination (Harrison and van Hoek, 2008). This has further resulted in an evolution of cross functional models of logistics, integrating the companies' business processes.

This lends complexities to the logistics, especially due to fragmented supply channels, increasing service and product variations, consumer demand customizations, and host of other factors. This should not come as a surprise, and the researchers further inform that as the world becomes increasingly complex, due to ever changing modes of operations brought forth by innovations and enhancements in technologies, one must expect logistics to become more and more complex and challenging (Handfield *et al.*, 2013). The complexities are further complicated by customization demands from consumers, and this is for the logistics and supply-chain to enable the company to satisfy the varying consumer needs. Meeting customer demands is the foremost objective for any business and the logistics/supply-chain management. The researchers inform from their relevant study conducted on this context that companies regarded meeting this customers' demands as most important objective of their logistics and supply change management and improvement.

The researchers opine that this is also the major reason why the companies look ahead to improve upon the logistics and seek a better and effective supply chain links and networks. As it was already highlighted above that the logistics are getting challenging and complexities are adding-up to the already complicated operation, the ways are now being sought to optimize the whole set-up. Whilst many researchers now agree that innovations and performance improvement of logistics are required and have even directed their study and subject of the research towards recommending the areas of improvement, still there are many related areas which require considerable amount of research and study to propose the betterment of the overall management.

Another example or aspect, which the researchers have identified, is the *factorization of supply-chain or logistics on the inventory management*. One is well aware that companies employ a series of methodologies and process improvement, six sigma/lean techniques or advanced inventory management methods to maintain an optimal level of inventory. What is meant here is that all the internal factors are employed, even the demand and supply is also a parameter in determining and maintaining the inventory. But, not many evidences are available where the companies would actually find the impact of inventory levels on logistics (Holmström *et al.*, 2008). The authors inform that this technique of "automatic identification" can be employed to maintain dependable and robust levels of inventory.

There are many such examples and evidences from the past that although a technology was developed, and was proven and in place for some time, the underpinning research or study and recommendations, which could help other companies, as the researches are published and could be noticed by corporate world, were slow paced due to various reasons. Authors inform that associating a new technology with a research comes under the category of "explorative research" which is invariably time consuming and a risky proposition for many researchers (Matthiassen, 2002). Many researchers would rather prefer an easier or empirical way to assist their research and their areas of research would depend or rely on the existing models, so the authors opine that it takes its own time to publish the researches on innovative technologies, their applications and practice.

Thus, a major challenge is modelling the new research design; define, quantify and validate the underlying phenomenon, its parameters and variables, especially in the context of research on logistics and supply-chain. When new technologies emerge it is recommended by the authors to put this under evaluation to determine its efficacy, and for this it is recommended to develop at first an evaluation criteria (Simon, 1996). This can be further reinforced by developing the criteria as to how the research would be performed (Pickering, 1995).

With this backdrop, where the significance of logistics, its gradual evolution spanning decades, general evidence of lack of research in advanced areas in logistics and related research designs, and the need to develop the knowledge as recommended by the host of authors was highlighted, *now in the next section the background of the research as envisioned in this paper is presented.* So within this chapter of research which introduces the topic of research "Logistics of Industrial Enterprise", the next section begins with a brief overview of the background of the study. Following this, the primary purpose of this research, the aims and objectives are discussed.

Background of the research

Due to the increased competitions and the rapid changes in the consumer life-styles, the ways in which the business market operates has changed dramatically. As highlighted earlier, logistics, operations and supply-chain is becoming complex and harder day by day, and survival within this competitive market is a challenge for the business organization. Logistics, which was already highlighted as being regarded as a key business performance parameter by top enterprises, requires new adaptations and improvisations and this has become mandatory for the survival and competitive strategy for the business organization (Graham, 2004).

This research project is based on the Russian company called Kamaz. The report will discuss the organisation of the logistical systems prevailing at Kamaz, which is a manufacturing enterprise. The company manufactures tractor-trailers and has its characteristic supply chain management policy and sound logistics. It is believed that some companies in Russia are operating in a sub-optimal strategy as some of the finance and business experts within the companies opine that an optimisation of logistical/supply chain management policy is required. They debate that their company at times faces stiff challenges in delivering its products or deal with the customization as required by their clients and so an appropriate economic evaluation of effectiveness must be undertaken.

While some members in top management feel that although the same system of logistics and same network of supply-chain operates for years in their company and the company even experienced good revenues in the earlier years, but, they were not able to explain the decline in the revenues due to ever-increasing operating costs. Due to this some financial experts in the companies believed that the operating-costs were increasing due to the lack of optimization, research and innovation in logistics which should match with the development in logistics techniques and innovations. Their company had ignored the revamping of their logistic process despite the recommendation to the management based on the model adopted by some successful companies in Russia. As per the researchers, the companies in manufacturing sector in Russia, who took due diligence on predicting or forecasting accurately the parameters like required production, inventory levels required, forecasting cargo base, and so on, performed well (Fisenko, 2011).

Research Aim

To study the impact of logistics on the business performance and determine whether the profit margins could be improved by improving the quality of logistics.

Research Objectives

Russia has been traditionally using rail for shipping heavy machinery but Europe has been using roads. European Union is expanding towards former post-Soviet countries where rail is more developed than roads. The objective of this research is to analyse the optimisation of logistics for heavy goods. Formally the research objectives are stated as:

- To analyse the logistics approaches within the manufacturing enterprise which can have impact on the business performance and profit margins thereof;
- To analyse the impact of the relationship between a manufacturing enterprise and its contractors which can also have impact on the business performance;

- To assess the risks associated with logistics of the manufacturing enterprise which can degrade the profit margins, and measures to mitigate such risks;
- To propose an optimum solution as to how the logistics aspects and related technological innovations can help improve the business performance and increase the profit margins.

To summarize, profit margin is the most important aspect for businesses in general and logistics in particular. Incidentally 'profitability' figures as the keyword in Martin Christopher's definition of logistics:

"Logistics is the process of strategically managing the procurement, movement and storage of materials, parts and finished inventory (and the related information flows) through the organization and its marketing channels in such a way that current and future profitability are maximized through the cost-effective fulfillment of orders." (Christopher, 2011)

As the authors suggest, logistics is something which determines the movement of goods, products, semi-finished items, inventory, raw material, etc. from a source to destination, within the premises of the company or to external places, within the network or supply and distribution channels, in a way to maximize the profitability. They further suggest that the completion of the orders, which implicitly means customers' satisfaction,   must be achieved in a cost effective way, to maximize the profitability. Profitability is also dependent on many other aspects of the business, for instance, boosting sales with the improvement of customer relationships, and this can be achieved only through satisfied customers, and for which, again logistics play a vital role. Rushton et. al. (2010) dedicate much of their study on practical logistics issues that enable the maximization of profit, the minimization of costs and thus the improvement of ROI (Rushton *et al.*, 2010) (Return on investment): **ource***: The many ways in which logistics can provide an impact on an organization's return on investment.* (Rushton *et al.*, 2010)

Logistics is an important aspect because improper management of logistics might influence the profit margins (Prishchepov et al. 2013). It is apparent that optimisation of logistics is necessary in order to achieve the required or desired profit margins since shipping might be expensive (Zhukov 2012). So now the question arises, and which must be optimally answered, is that how does one ship or dispatch a trailer or goods from one part of world to another one, while maintaining, or even maximizing, the profit margins? This is the key question, even for this research, which needs to be analyzed and ascertained, since logistics are expensive (Stickley et al. 2013)due to the sheer size or weight of the products or the distances which must be covered are extensive.

The importance and impact of logistics is phenomenal to the organization. For one, it provides the "competitive advantage" – a positional of supremacy over the competitors, and makes the company the customers' favourite. This phenomenon is explained by the researcher in a 3-way relationship: (Christopher, 2011)

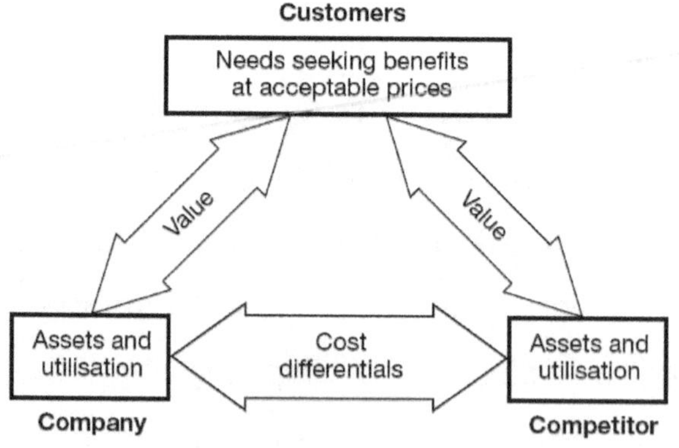

The 3-way relation exists between the Company, customer and competitor. Customer would always try to seek the advantage, as informs the author. But, the smart company would look at the logistics to reduce its costs, improve the timings of delivery and at the same time try to maximize its profits. As it was highlighted above, winning back customers and improving the customer relations boost sales and profits, as opined by the researchers. However, the logistics still plays a key role in generating the company's revenue.

Explaining Objectives and their elaboration in Research context

The principal object of this research is to investigate the logistics of manufacturing enterprise in Russia. Therefore, investigation is focussed to the Russian manufacturing industries in general, and specifically illustrating the examples from the company called Kamaz Logistics and studying their operations in the research context. The logistics company has been one of the oldest one, and perhaps the only major firm, manufacturing trailers in the region. Russia being a huge country, logistics plays a very significant role to effectively distribute heavy goods, like trailers, across the country and elsewhere outside the country for exports. In the global context, Russia has one of the highest Logistics Costs, as shown in the figure below. Russia is one of the topmost countries having the huge amount of expenditures in logistics, which heavily affects rate of goods-production, reduces trades efficiencies, adversely affects healthy competition amongst the companies and affects the country's economy (RosBusinessConsulting, 2011). Hence, as stated in a research, the share of logistics costs in Russia's gross domestic product exceeds a whopping 20 per cent, which is not only the highest among the BRICS (Brazil, Russia, India, China and South Africa) Countries, but is too high even at Global Standards, as represented in the bar graph shown below:

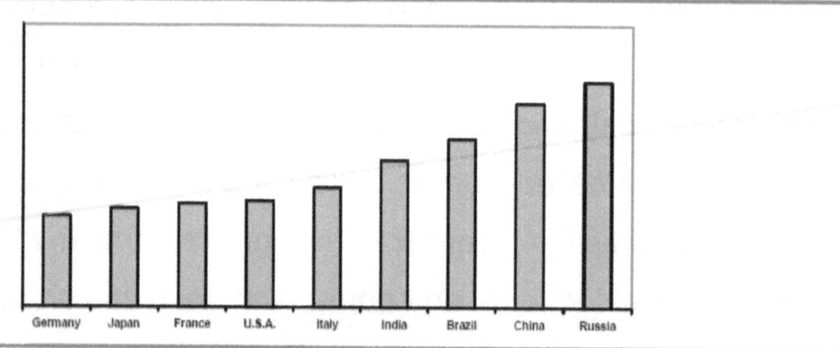

Source: **Logistics costs in different countries of the world and Russia, 2009, % of GDP.** (Armstrong & Associates, 2013)

Logistics is a branch in the tree or network of supply chain management, which pertains to the deliveries, and distribution of goods, products or even services(Genchev 2009). This means that delivery & distribution of goods is getting affected, and this is mainly due to tremendous distances but poor quality of Russian roads to support the movement, irrational distribution & availability of several of the manufacturing infrastructure, and archaic age-old set-up of cargo deliveries from manufacturing site to consumers with ineffective internal logistics in general (RosBusinessConsulting, 2011).

To effectively plan and control the logistics processes and to manage them internally within the company and coordinate across a huge country like Russia and its various regions, it is necessary to accurately forecast the relevant factors, for instance, forecasting cargo-base, understanding and generating multi modal transport-network or the network of supply chain, forecasting required investment, forecasting production, predicting direction and rate of the science and technical advancement and innovation, and so on (Fisenko, 2011).*Hence, the aim for this research is at first to understand the existing processes of logistics within this Kamaz enterprise, and since this company, as the Russian area itself, is one of the largest logistics company, so their experience* can be taken over, understood and compared with companies in other regions, within Russians as well as some successful companies globally located, who ship heavy machinery. The model adopted by Kamaz can be compared and contrasted with few other successful companies which produce heavy machinery and employ their distinct model of Logistics/Supply-chain Management, and generalize the findings to propose an optimized and highly-probable Logistic model of success, leading to business improvement and profitability, especially in Russian context.

To accurately forecast on the parameters as stated above, so as to *effectively plan and control the logistics processes, one also needs to understand* Russia's characteristic shipment strategy in logistics, associated with the tractor-trailer. Russia is the benchmark in logistics associated with the tractor-trailer (Posternakova, 2012). This is because most of the Russian shipment is being pursued either via rail or through air. The roads in Russia have a poor general condition as highlighted from the sources (RosBusinessConsulting, 2011). Train is better means of commuting and shipping goods across the country. This research is required because shipping in many other countries is pursued through land (roads) since this appears to be easier. Rail logistics is not so developed in many countries as in Russia and US. Therefore, it is necessary to establish how rail logistics can benefit people and businesses (Tuominen, 2009). Russia has developed its approaches due to its size and lack of roads however Europe prefers roads due to simplicity. Furthermore, there are quite a number of roads in UK allowing the logistics companies to ship via land. It shall be reiterated that road logistics suffer from mobility since they need to be closed down when big or dangerous goods are transferred (ITS Russia, 2013). It would be much simpler to use the rail network to ship big goods like tractor trailers allowing people to use motorways effectively and not closing them or slowing the traffic down.

Another importance of the Rail logistics is that it supports and even extends the Supply-Chain Network of heavy industries, to reach out to more customers, as whilst the agricultural industries or software firm could be set-up easily anywhere, even at the vicinity of new sources of raw materials or factors of production, it is not very easy to set-up many heavy industries. Therefore, it is important to understand the ways towards the effectiveness of logistics related to heavy goods.

Processes need to be improvised, to facilitate long distance service, and capitalize on the efficient modes of movements of goods, in order to make logistics more effective. There are certain definite advantages of setting the best foot forward, and the way the model company has excelled, must be analysed and compared with other companies. Based on this, the attempt would be made to recommend the improvement for logistics processes within a manufacturing enterprise which may set an example to allow companies, even in other countries, to "take-away" from the Russian experience of effective rail logistics services. At least this part of the Russian Logistics System, it is believed, has adapted from innovations and offers efficient and most cost-effective solutions (Yug Logistics, 2013). Source: (Yug Logistics, 2013)

This is effective for shipping big goods preventing from any disturbances that can be seen in land logistics. Western European countries have always tried to build good roads and to use them as the main means for logistics. However, Eastern European Countries are joining the European Union which used to be in the Soviet Union and they have inherited Russian traditions not to focus on roads but to build rail networks. *As per the research from Pricewatercoopers*, Russia is huge, and as the below statistics reveal, has tremendous potential, and the proposed model can serve as an example for not only Russian companies but the companies located outside Russia *Transportation and Logistics* (PWC, 2013).

Source: *Transportation and Logistics. Pricewatercoopers.* (PWC, 2013)*http://www.pwc.com/en_gx/gx/transportation-logistics/tl2030/emerging-markets/pdf/tl2030_vol3_final.pdf*

Coming to this proposed company Kamaz, which has been chosen for this research has the installed capability to produce tractors trailers for agricultural purposes. The company produces over 50,000 units of massive trailers each year, and as highlighted, even this company has its distinct logistics and supply chain management policy to serve their network of customers. Companies in Supply-Chain/Logistics have their own Delivery rules to allow them to meet their own goals and to try and improve their performance by implementing strategic decisions(Banai & Weisberg 2003).

Logistics permeates all functions and departments of the enterprise for the purpose of optimizing a stream for materials, information and financial flows(Aastrup 2003). The authors further opine that the logistics necessitates a considerable amount of strategic planning and requires a lot of pondering in order to channelize new resources in optimizing their operations. The crux and the critical approach here is to achieve the optimization in strategic areas. The ultimate approach is towards the optimization of all processes related to the organization of production in order to achieve their goals (Khajavi et al. 2014). But, in the research context, and within the context of selected region and company, it is important to appreciate the ways in which the logistics parameters could be optimised in order to improve the profit margins of the business related to agriculture. In this research context, there is not much evidence of previous research that

European logistics companies are aware of shipping big machinery goods via rail permitting people to use the motorways without disruptions.

Some companies need to revamp their logistics management, improve services and reduce costs, and for this they must acquire awareness of the many different facets of logistics and the supply chain. As the researchers Rushton et. al. (2010) suggest that they may still not be very clear as to how to manage their logistics in best possible way, and hence they could experience reduction in profits or even incur some financial losses due to this lack of understanding or sub-optimal way of operating (Rushton *et al.*, 2010).Due to good conditions of the roads, the authors say that it has become customary or a culture that, for instance, European companies tend to use roads as a primary means of transport in supply-chain network, despite the fact that road transport is the costliest affair:

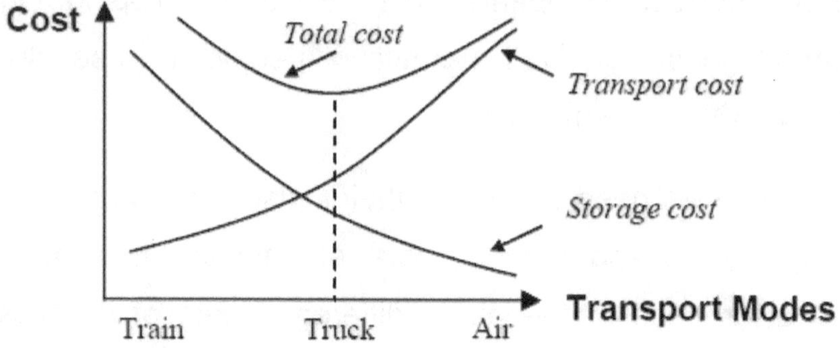

Source: Transport patterns and total costs (Chang, 1998)

As shown in the graph, Train is the cheapest mode of transport and there is one added advantage to it. But, there are other factors as well in the transport systems, which lend a fair degree of complexity to the logistics and supply change management. The cost calculation is not as direct and apparent as it may appear, but, it involves a considerable amount of research, analyses, estimations, forecast and recommendations. Some researchers suggest that even though the recommendations have been made, and the company starts operating optimally, but, the system must again be re-evaluated every five years at least or at some other ideal frequency (TSENG *et al.*, 2005). This is the reason that the research on logistic topics is necessary. It is possible that in some cases the road transport is cheaper for some companies at some regions, but mostly it is observed that the motorways could be shut during transportation of big goods and the traffic is slowed down and congested whereas rail shipping does not cause any such problems. Therefore, it is essential to advance current state of the knowledge in logistics and it is recommendable to introduce an effective option for rail opportunities, and this aspect is worth analyzing. Thus, as it was highlighted a novel approach is intended to be developed in this thesis to give an insight into the optimisation of the logistics processes.

A company can be successful only on the basis of system optimisation of the complex software processes and other production as well as marketing techniques, which all form the basis of modern logistic processes within the organisation of movement of material and information flows(Liao & Kao 2014). Such attributes as marketing techniques, relationships with suppliers and relationship with customers are believed to have impact of logistics and the quality of production. It will be discussed how to optimise and improve these aspects to achieve better logistics solutions. One is aware that most operations, techniques, processes, customer relations, logistics management, supply channels, and host of attributes are different for each business, and no matter how similar the product or service line of two companies seem equivalent, but, there are a lot of factors and parameters which can make a world of difference. It was highlighted that even in logistics context, some companies are successful, like the example company Kamaz but others failed to survive and succumbed to the load of logistics. So the company Kamaz, which is flourishing needs to be researched and the resulting findings and analyses could be further presented and the model of success proposed along with their approach. This model and experience can then be considered to be applied to other similar companies.

Lastly, in this section, it would not be inappropriate to express the significance of people management, and their relationship which is of paramount importance, since the business can depend on supplier relationships and it is always human resource management which matters to some extent. The objective in this research will also be to analyze the impact of human relationship between the contractors, suppliers and consumers with the company and to evaluate their significance(Wagner & Sutter 2012).

Literature review

Various scientific, humanities and business research papers have been considered and perused to extend the knowledge and the scope of this research.

What is Logistics?

Logistics is a business process which involves multiple departments in its operations and so it cuts across functional boundaries and expects the required contribution from each department. Logistics is the process of strategically managing the procurement, movement and storage of materials, parts and finished inventory (and the related information flows) through the organization and its marketing channels in such a way that current and future profitability are maximized through the cost-effective fulfillment of orders." (Christopher, 2011). Daskin interprets logistics as "the design and operation of the physical, managerial, and informational systems needed to allow goods to overcome time and space" (Daskin, 1992). Another source, The Council of Logistics Management, promulgates logistics as "the process of planning, implementing, and controlling the efficient, cost-effective flow and storage of raw materials, in-process inventory, finished goods and related information from point of origin to point of consumption for the purpose of conforming to customer requirements". In the past, logistics had a variety of names such as "physical distribution", "business logistics", "supply chain", and so forth. However, "logistics management" is the most widely accepted term among professionals (LambertD. and Stock, 1993).

A framework of Logistics in literature

The framework of the integrated logistics system presented in some logistics research literature involves the system's major components, their relationships and operating philosophies (Chiu, 1995). This framework delineates some special characteristics and several important issues existing in the logistics management system, the system's major components and their integrative operations, and the use of information technology. This framework is pragmatic in nature and will present performance analysis and improvement suggestions that are helpful to logistics practitioners (Chiu, 1995). Over the last years, the traditional logistics systems have evolved the broader strategic approaches of distribution management. The article (Tan 2001)attempts to clearly describe logistics and the framework and also covers various strategies and the conditions conductive to logistics within the

(Tan 2001).In a similar literature, the author presents a representation of subsystems and flows in within a framework of a logistic information system. (Chiu, 1995) <u>Source</u>: A framework of a logistic information system. (Chiu, 1995)

This framework is appropriate to the research objectives of the current paper, as the model within the framework, which is envisaged as the outcome of this research, envisions producing business performance improvement. A model which enlightens and illuminates the path to achieve competitive advantage surely adds a value to a business organization and serves as a good business proposition (Reck and Long, 1988). One model will be attempted in this research as the domain, here, is also not limited to a region and the research also has global perspective. The strategic purchasing as shown in logistics can be influenced by the global factors. This is the reason that many more purchasing professionals are now trained in cross-functional areas and strategic elements of the competitive strategy (Reck and Long, 1988).

Based on the points which were discussed above, a SWOT Analysis is proposed

There are certain issues characteristic to the logistics, which are unique and distinct from Supply chain Management. So what is the difference between Supply Chain Management and Logistics? The term 'Supply Chain Management' was originally introduced by consultants in the early 1980s and has subsequently gained tremendous attention. Supply Chain Management was viewed as logistics outside the businesses to include suppliers and customers. Logistics always represented a supply chain orientation from point of origin to point of consumption. Logistics is a functional system within the business and is a greater concept that interacts with the management of information flows and materials across the supply chain(Lambert & Cooper 2000).

Logistics is that part of the supply chain process that implements, plans and controls the effective and efficient flow and storage of products, services and related information from the original point to the consumption point in order to meet customer's requirements (Lambert & Cooper 2000).

Researchers inform that the methodology of Supply Chain Management consists of four main elements: (1) Supply chain assessment, (2) Supply chain redesign, (3)Supply chain control, and (4) Continuous supply chain improvement.(Vrijhoef & Koskela 2000). However, the researchers clearly mention logistics consists and signifies more on satisfied customers, economies of operations, capacity to serve more orders and improved business performance (Wim Bosman Russia, 2013). Adapting the New logistic technologies allow improve the process of cargo delivering and increasing customer demands push the logistic industry forward (Efimova and Tsenzharik, 2009). Whilst this synergy exists between companies' performance, increasing customer demands and growth of the logistic industries itself, and these are inter-related phenomena, but, the principle aim of the current research would focus on studying the impact of logistics on the business performance and determine whether the profit margins would be improved by improving the quality of logistics.

Reviews on Third-party logistics (3PL) providers and their relevance to Research

In the final portion of the previous section it was concluded from the studies so far that it was not inappropriate to express the significance of people management, and their relationship which is of paramount importance, since the business can depend on supplier relationships and it is always human resource management which matters to some extent. On the similar lines, is the importance of the relationship between third party logistic providers (3PL) and the company(Wagner & Sutter 2012). The objective in this research will also be to analyze the impact of such relationship between the providers, contractors, suppliers and consumers with the company and to evaluate their significance. However, as the author suggest in their research, that in spite of the challenges of creating innovation in third-party logistics provider-customer relationships, little is known about how such relationships can be engaged by customers and providers in joint innovation projects and the benefits that can be obtained from such innovation activities. There are contingency factors, as the literature highlights, that are important in customer-provider relationships. Such contingency factors are -- high integration with customer, complementary relationship-specific investments, establishing links to customers insisting on new services, agreement of benefit sharing, and these have impact on the joint third-party logistics provider-customer innovation projects. *Innovation projects allow the providers to renew their positions, strengthen relationships with customers and attain higher performance. Thus, Logistics services can be a source of sustainable competitive advantage*(Wagner & Sutter 2012).

There is an increasing need to the evaluation of the theory used in order to constitute a solid base for future development of the field of study, as opined by the researchers(Karatas-Cetin & Denktas-Sakar 2013). Therefore, due diligence has been given by the researchers and in the current research, to highlight the relations and relevance between the theories, practice and the research methods employed in logistics discipline. As will be analyzed in great detail in the next section of this paper, which pertains to research methodology, it is appropriate to highlight the excerpts from the literature on business research methods, the importance of understanding the underlying theories on the subject matter of research and their application to actual practice (Saunders *et al.*, 2007). The authors highlight in this literature in great detail about the methods in which the research should be carried and the importance of developing the research model so that it is applicable and useful in practice.

ualitative inquiries in logistics

The research methods, as highlighted by the researchers, could be either qualitative or quantitative (Rajasekar,

Philominathan, & Chinnathambi, 2013). The qualitative research is more towards pragmatic approach and interpretivism as shown in the above figure and is concerned with such qualities as reliability and validity. This research approach for logistics interprets to ascertaining credibility, transferability, conformability and dependability which are all qualitative attributes (Aastrup 2003).

These attributes will be established through the methods as elaborated in the next section, with the goal to establish the research quality and the resulting criteria's role in logistics. A basic assumption is the recognition of several trends in the logistics discipline that indicate a departure from the traditional quantitative positivistic paradigm towards multi-paradigmatic research efforts and interpretivism which include the use of a variety of qualitative research methods. It is suggested by researchers in logistics, that when dealing with certain soft issues of logistics one should consider and benefit from these alternative criteria (Aastrup 2003).

Role of education on logistics & supply chain management to Professional manager

Finally, it is not surprising to get references in the logistics research to the role of education on logistics & supply chain management to Business managers and executive(Erturgut &

Soysekerci 2011). The logistics is an inter-disciplinary field and is very much related to business administration and management. Supply Chain Management also includes the logistic and the reverse logistic operations and is capable to become an academic discipline on its own, as suggested in the literature. Sauders et. al. (2007) have suggested the importance of application side or practice of an academic research, which adds value to the companies in their operations (Saunders *et al.*, 2007). So, it becomes critical for the professional managers to receive Logistic and SCM education and training to help them and understand, assimilate, ascertain and implement the recommendations from such research. In this research, the importance and necessity of Logistic and SCM education for the Professional managers are emphasized. Thus, a number of recommendations and suggestions regarding the significance of logistic and SCM education in terms of mandatory education and their importance have been put forward, based on this literature(Erturgut & Soysekerci 2011).

Methodology

This chapter consists of the overall methodology that will be used to conduct the research. Methodology comprises of all the activities that are required to conduct the study and generate it into a report.

The new knowledge is proposed to be developed which follows the objective of the research using the research methodology in a systematic way and offer the recommendations. There are certain well defined steps that are proposed to be followed in a sequential manner to achieve the final answer to the research aim. The research purpose, methods and strategy of the research have already been introduced earlier and will be explained in this chapter in the context of research methodology.

Methods used in this project

It is important to establish what methods will be used in this project in order to pursue the research and to attain pre-set goals. For the avoidance of doubt, this shall be reiterated that the purpose of this project is to research the Russian logistics services employed in shipping heavy and big products by rail and to propose an optimisation for the European logistics companies which have been historically using roads as the logistics means; however, the European Union is expanding towards post-Soviet countries where rail was more preferred than logistics. There are drawbacks of roads such as closure of motorways which considerably affects people's life and turns out to become a waste of time for travellers.

Qualitative research is the most appropriate approach in this thesis since it involves data collection such as historical research, philosophical research and grounded theory. It is apparent that the business models of many logistics companies are built on historical facts as it has been mentioned before. The historical facts are that rail is the main means in Russia and former Soviet Union, which historically remains until now in many former Soviet republics. Furthermore, said former Soviet republics such as Lithuania, Latvia and Estonia have joined the European Union. The logistics companies in these Baltic countries prefer to use rail for shipping goods since they used to be in the Soviet Union where historically rail has been playing a vital role since Tsar's time. It is necessary to investigate the historical reasons of rail and to link them with current situation allowing to introduce the technologies for advancing current state of the art logistics services.

In logistics domain, there are many circumstances which entail the use of qualitative research interviews as only methodology of data-collection which is beneficial. These situations are as follows::

• the purpose of the research – which is exploratory

• the necessity and the significance of establishing personal contact;

• the nature of the data collection questions which are complex and open-ended

• length of time required and completeness of the process is long as logistics is a complex process (Saunders *et al.*, 2007)

About Company Kamaz

KAMAZ(Камский автомобильный завод–КАМАЗ/Kamskiy avtomobilny zavod) – or: Kamaz Automobile Plant is the Russia's truck-trailer manufacturer based out of Naberezhnye Chelny, Tatarstan, Russia. KAMAZ started its operations in 1976. It is the largest manufacturer of heavy-duty trailer models, which are even exported to several parts within the

Globe, like Eastern Europe, South American countries, China, Middle-East & North Africa (MENA). Their trailers and truckers are so robust and match winning that in the Dakar Rally they have won a record 12 number of times. Incidentally, KAMAZ is not only the largest producer of trailers in Russia, but also the largest producer in CIS. The Trailer manufacturer produces almost 93,600 trucks-trailers annually which means 260 trucks/trailers in one day.("Новости. ОАО "КАМАЗ"". www.Kamaz.net.) Modified KAMAZ trucks/vehicles are also employed by the army of Russian. Kamaz has always been the largest manufacturer of trailers in Russia and the Soviet Union. The company has developed its production portfolio since its foundation and the trailers for regular vehicles were produced in 80s.

It is interesting that it is one of the most major companies in Russia who manufacture trailers and ship them across the country and outside of Russia. The shipping costs are quite high due to the distance and remote places. Russian Federation is the biggest country in the world and it is lacking in roads in some areas however it is known that the Russian rail network in the best one in the world along with the American rail networks. It is apparent that is it probably impractical to ship trailers via air because trailers are massive in size and heavy in weight. However, trailers can be shipped via rail using freight carriages. The company uses mainly the Trans-Siberian rail as a principle means of transport in their logistics, and a detailed study would further reveala clear understanding of their logistics strategies and the supply chain management efficiencies.

The vast majority of entrepreneurs sooner or later face important challenges such as the delivery of goods to the consumer. Historically, the share of rail transport in the Russian Federation was more than forty percent of all freight (Cai et al. 2013). In addition, certain categories of goods can be delivered exclusively by rail in many regions of the country (Aastrup 2003).

With all the obvious advantages the delivery of goods by rail has a number of features. Understanding of all the nuances of this process untrained a person quite in a difficult way. The ignorance of basic rules and norms entails a consequence, costs, moral and financial losses.

Optimise all processes as to how to organize the international rail freight and these tasks incur logistics within the company.

Logistics is the science of monitoring, planning and management of transportation, storage of goods such as raw materials, their processing and delivery of the final product to the consumer. Besides material things logistics is engaged in storage, transmission and processing of information on these shipments.

Transport logistics connects all parts of the transportation process into a single chain such as selection of the optimal route, or several types of transport (multimodal transport), preparation of necessary documents (including customs), the organization of loading and unloading and other logistics company takes over the functions of single operator responsible for the entire transportation process from design to unloading at destination. On request, the company organizes cargo insurance, warehousing services, security services, registration at customs , etc.

The goal of any logistics company is very clearly expressed in the rule of logistics, namely the necessary cargo requires the quality of the required quantity, which should occur at the right time, being delivered to the right place, at the right cost. The cost must me minimal since customers want to have a minimal cost whereas suppliers want to keep the cost minimal. However, logistics companies wish to boost the costs of shipping and to make their profits. So there are three parties: a suppliers, a customer and a logistics company who ships. It is also possible to have to parties: a supplier and a customer; in this case a supplier would have its own transportation services.

It is unclear which option is cheaper and better for the profit margin: to have three or two parties within the supply chain management, i.e. logistics. If trailers are delivered via rail rather than via road, then probably it is better to ship them via a third party since it might be difficult to have a private train in the absence of roads in Russia.

Project scope

A Russian company called Kamaz, manufacturing trailers and Trucks that would be used in fields for agricultural and miscellaneous other purposes, will be analysed in this report.

Research Purpose

The purpose is to optimise the significant factors of logistics to form a perfect model of supply chain management.

Research Design

Research design is a blueprint or a detailed plan for how a research study is to be completed. Based on the purpose of research, researches can be classified into four categories (Collis & Hussey, 2003) -- Exploratory Research, Descriptive Research, Analytical Research and Predictive Research.. As it was already stated that the current research is more on the qualitative side, so the current research is exploratory in nature. The research topic is already formed and formally the topic is reiterated as under:

"Logistics of Industrial Enterprise".

The research objectives have also been stated clearly and not this research must answer and fulfill the objectives of the research. The research process will be iterative in nature and at each iteration the newly acquired learning would reflect on the research ideas continually, and the research and the methodologies could be tweaked as required. Some of the research sections can also be revised at some stage if felt appropriate, and it is during the final or concluding stages of the research that one can expect the final version of research findings and recommendations. The iterative research process to be followed is represented as hereunder:

Data collection is required for any qualitative and quantitative research. This research will be pretty much qualitative, as already stated above, and the author has collected some primary data from company which are published on company's website.

Besides that, the researcher will also conduct some secondary research which will included academic journals, books and other literature. As far as the methodology is concerned, the author adopts from the "Onion" of research which displays several layers, wherein the peripheral layer is the overall research methodology a researcher will adopt. The research philosophy of Interpretivism was highlighted and the researcher adopts this as initial layer. The research is more on qualitative and inductive approach, and the remaining layers would be compatible with this approach. So as the researcher peels another layer of the "onion", the analysis and data collection would require the adoption of compatible strategy (Johnson and Clark 2006). The use of qualitative methods in the form of case studies would be used to create an in-depth and rich account (Yin 2003;Scholz and Tietje 2002; Rubin and Rubin 1995) of how the company has employed the efficient and cost effective logistics strategy and deployed best possible Supply Chain Network, where many companies in the same area of operations have failed to generate even a fair amount of profitability. The data collection will be done from the primary resources of the main logistic company (Kamaz) and from the other companies. Since it is qualitative research, so the questionnaires will be more on exploratory side of the research, open ended questions and will also include actual behavior of the management as well as 'how' and 'why' the strategies were used. It will also require a brief data analysis of the comparisons and ANNOVA, regression and t-test analysis using some statistical package, like IBM's SPSS.

Research Ethics

Like all the ideal researches, this research has also followed to maintain the professional ethical standards. Research ethics is operated in all companies differently or similarly depending on their location and the nature of their business. Honesty in data collection and analysis was done without changing any data. During analysis, proper care was taken. No personal questions or ethnic background should be taken into account. No nationality or ethnical background of postmen should be considered as they are irrelevant. Furthermore, consideration of these aspects may discriminate against groups of people leading to the breach of the European law associated with human rights. Company's internal system will be investigated by way of reviewing the resources available online. The data is available on their website and has been made public. It does not seem that there will be any issues with the Data Protection Act as no personal data will be needed.

Chapter 4

Organisation of logistics enterprise

It is vital and crucial to consider the logistics at manufacturing enterprise. The significance of logistics will be discussed in this chapter in the context of the research objectives. It is apparent that manufacturing enterprise use a special approach for meeting their goals and succeeding in their supply chain management decisions (Roh et al. 2014).

The following sections will be covered in this chapter.

1. **Operating fields of logistics at manufacturing enterprise**

There are five main fields of logistics at any, or most, manufacturing enterprise. They are purchasing, production, distribution, transport and information. To perform any logistics action, a supplier should be found to enable the enterprise to purchase a product. Suppliers may have various products hence production needs to be considered. Delivery is the key in logistics thus the enterprise will focus over the distribution. Various transportation means can be considered when delivery is concerned. Company may use national or private transportation services. However, some companies have their own logistics departments and they perform their own transportation services. Information has always been the key in any matter. The largest companies like Kamaz also consider rail as their important means in their arrangement of logistics.

Within the manufacturing enterprise, there are several operational fields that must be considered. One of the foremost consideration for them is the Logistics outsourcing. For the companies like Kamaz, it is the most vital and crucial consideration for planning their strategy for logistics as the involve Rail transport, which needs to be outsourced. Within the Outsourcing itself, there are several operational fields which need to be considered. Basically, there are 4 operational fields:

a. Transportation
b. Freight Forwarding
c. Warehousing
d. Logistics Management

The nature of involvement and participation of the individual fields in the structure can be represented as follows:

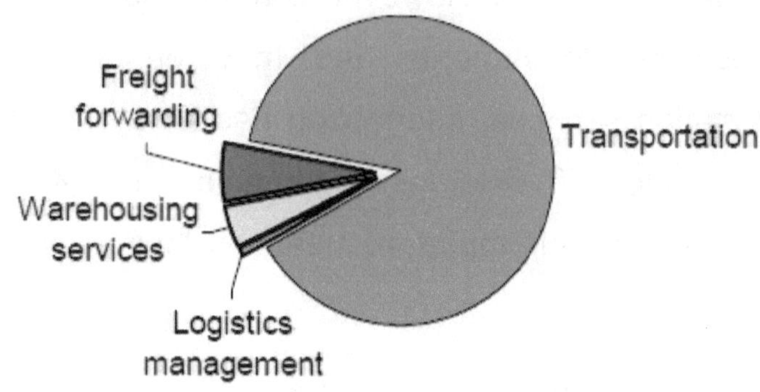

Source: Structure of the operational fields in Logistics (RosBusinessConsulting, 2011)

For a company like Kamaz, Transportation is the major component in the logistics arrangement. Transporting Trailers across the country naturally involves major cost and involvement. This is the most important field and major focus must be given on optimizing this field. Related to this field is the need of warehousing services and it accounts for the time between the manufacturing and actual shipping of the manufactured products. Similarly there is impact on the costs

accordingly as shown in the below figure: Source: Cost
component: (RosBusinessConsulting, 2011)

Hence the actual transportation is the major component of the
Total Costs of Operations (TOC) in logistics. Freight and
Warehousing are the next significant fields and they involve
such activities as cost of lease of storage space in commercial
use, operating expenses and cost of safekeeping services.
Safekeeping accounts for the safeguarding of the product
from the time of dispatch to the time of final delivery to the
buyer. It may also include insurance costs which covers the
risks of damages in transit.

The major aspect of interest in this research comes from the
fact that there is a fair degree of competition in the Russian
transport and logistics services. The key players are the third
party services (3PL) segment which is from the providers and
top players from the western logistics companies. These
companies have extensive experience in providing the
services especially to the majority of manufacturing and
product companies across the global. It is understood that
their extent of servicing and operations globally as well as in
the Rusian market is based on the activities, growth and
number of business transactions of their main customers in
Russia. As per the measured estimates from the data of

companies retrieved from the National Credit Bureau, the revenues of TOP transportation and logistics companies account for billion dollar roubles (National Credit Bureau). Here is the actual figure from the same source which provides the estimates of the actual revenues of these companies: *References: The data for foreign logistics operators include the revenues of companies registered in Russia and filing financial statements under Russian standards, translated into US dollars at the annual average exchange rate. Sources: Companies' data, National Credit Bureau, RBC. research estimate* (National Credit Bureau, 2010)

From this data it is clear that the Logistic Outsourcing is the major factor which brings the competitive edge to the manufacturing enterprise utilizing their services. This is the reason that a proper weight must be assigned to this field or variable to optimize the logistics costs. Some companies out-source the activities after proper analyses to reduce the costs. Economies of scale help to reduce the costs in total operations. 3PL companies have large scale volume in business transactions of identical activities. For instance, their role could be just to facilitate the transfer of trailers or heavy vehicles through rail from Place a to Place B. The bulk transactions help them to optimize their operations, and therefore costs, and carry forward this saving to their client, so as to be competitive in their own category of 3PL providers. In this was, a smart manufacturing enterprise like Kamaz seeks this opportunity to reduce its own Total cost of Operations (TCO) as for them also the major component in costs is transportation.

Thus, we see that how the various factors help in reducing the costs and whilst some companies increase the margin of their profits, others carry forward their savings to customers, as Sales price is one of the decisive parameters affecting the Sales.

2. Significance of supply chain in manufacturing logistics

Significance of supply chain on the logistics of the manufacturing enterprise is also one factor which merits the mention in this chapter and worth its consideration with respect to research object of optimizing the logistics function. While in the previous section we considered the effect of the variables and their operationalization for the purpose of research analysis, here we undertake some exploratory research and quality of some suppliers and the modes they operate, which can have a bearing on the overall logistics strategy for the manufacturing enterprise. The two functions of logistics and supply chain are quite interconnected as shown in the below figure, where the circle represents the manufacturing enterprise, and the impacts are received from the customer focus and information technology. The management function in logistics integration and supply Network coordination has its bearing on Supplier and Buyer performance and reaction: Source: Logistics Integration and effects of supply chain. (Chen and Paulraj, 2004)

Customer Focus and Buyer's reaction in turn has the bearing on the optimization of the logistics function and this works pretty much as a chain. Again this is an interrelated phenomena and lends a fair degree of complexity and an object of research. Smart organization take this as a challenge and after careful analyses and study optimize this whole cycle by changing that aspect which adds more value. For instance, some organizations would take the help of information technology to automate this process itself and there are various solutions and models of IT Software in Logistics and supply chain (Chen and Paulraj, 2004). One example of such software is Oracle's Logistics and Supply chain Management Solution.

The theoretical foundation which has been provided here is fairly comprehensive and as shown in the figure, has many facets and should definitely assist in reaching the goal of competitiveness and this would definitely assist in creating and evaluating the propose research model as envisaged. Whilst this illustration of theoretical foundation of Internal Logistics and the effects of Supply chain opens new vistas to the subject, it also highlights the optimization of not only internal supply chain but also the importance of optimized external factors, and thereby the internal logistics within the manufacturing enterprise (Chen and Paulraj, 2004). The consequent outcome results in the creation of the proposed research model which is so comprehensive that it should ultimately help in rendering logistics process optimization. We also propose to using a software to enter the parameters of the model and evaluate the model with the various inputs and variables as discussed so far.

3. Significance of Railroads in logistics management

Significance of Railways on logistics will be covered in this section. Manufacturing enterprise will be taken as the basis for this section and thorough research in all aspects of

Railroads on logistics will be discussed. Any associated risks will and mitigation will also be discussed and researched (Takata & Yamanaka 2013). In this category of rail-road transport, there is a significant contribution of 3PLs. There are major players in Rail logistics in Russia, who provide innovative rail transport solutions. They are the specialists for railroad services within private sector and collaborate with the state railways for their clients from manufacturing and industrial sector. They would select their carrier as per their customer's business requirement to bring forth optimization in the performance and lower freight charges.

They can provide individualized support and render personal touch to their services for the transport needs. Thus, these 3PL Logistics provide rail services rendering the rail shipping less complex, simple, more efficient and more cost-effective. Their services get aligned with various rail-logistics initiative which makes their customers' operations more optimized and competitive (Yug Logistics, 2013). Source: Railroad Logistics: (Yug Logistics, 2013)

Thus, these companies can manage the railways services, together with freight and fleet management as a single-point and convenient service and cost-effective. They can monitor & control the transportation even across and throughout

Russian Federation, Turkey, Central Asia, Europe and even other countries. This can mean anything and everything to their customer --from tracking, tracing, and managing local or inter-national, to planning & scheduling their consignment , to controlling receiving and dispatching. Their Service-Centres provide supportive and information services and manage every aspect of movement of goods service. Thus, they specialize in the provisioning of transport service through private sector haulage. This all signifies an even better and efficient rail transport service which provides the competitive edge over other means of transport.